INTRODUCING WILD DELAWARE

John A. Hughes

John A. Hughes is secretary of the Delaware Department of
Natural Resources and Environmental Control.

I suppose that everyone of a certain age feels that they have lived in a transitional time, for only change is constant, yet my memories of Sussex County, Delaware, of the late '40s and '50s truly seem of a different era, one certainly wilder than present times, and that is why this book is an important one, because it is redolent of a bygone time.

It seems like a dream to me now, from being sent by my father down to the Lewes & Rehoboth Canal to catch a dozen soft-shell crabs for dinner from underneath the fallen trees, to anchoring at the center of the confluence of the canal and Rehoboth Bay to catch a bushel of fat hard shells for that night's feast — the equivalent nowadays to parking in the center lane of I-95.

As a child, from an unending supply of native fauna, I found it not at all unusual to accumulate a pet crow, 26 box turtles at once in a side yard pen, baby raccoons and foxes, blacksnakes, bats and one beautiful copperhead. Thanks to a mother who considered entertaining these unpredictable guests a normal part of child rearing, I acquired a working knowledge of wild Delaware, one glorious animal at a time. I haven't seen 26 box turtles all together in the last 10 years, a factor of development and traffic, I suspect. I'm still a patsy for any orphaned or injured animal and am lucky to have a wife who shares my mother's beneficent instincts. My childhood and my early career as a zookeeper at the National Zoo in Washington, D.C., have left me with an undying love of the wild, and while I respect the hunting ethic (hunters, perhaps because of their exposure to the wild, are by and large excellent conservationists), I can't conceive of killing any thing much larger than a greenhead fly.

These and dozens of other personal recollections remind me of a lost Delaware and I count myself fortunate to have lived in my own personal transitional time when such a wildness is part of my certain memory.

Fortunately, all of Delaware's wildness is not gone. Throughout our three counties, we have preserved some of our most precious wild places, in the form of 106,266 acres of parks, natural areas, and fresh and salt wetlands, some managed by state, county and local governments and others by conservation organizations.

And, as we've learned through our conservation efforts, lands no longer farmed have an amazing capacity for recovery and can return to flourishing habitats in a single human lifetime.

Indeed, we have come to see the fruits of our conservation initiatives. As a boy, I remember seeing only one eagle; ospreys were rare and pelicans were unheard of. Their numbers are far greater today.

Yes, there is still a wild Delaware. Kevin Fleming's patience has found it and his art and skill have preserved it forever in this glorious and evocative book. He gives us an opportunity to see what a lifetime of casual observation could never reveal — the wonder of Delaware's natural resources viewed through the caring eye of a true artist.

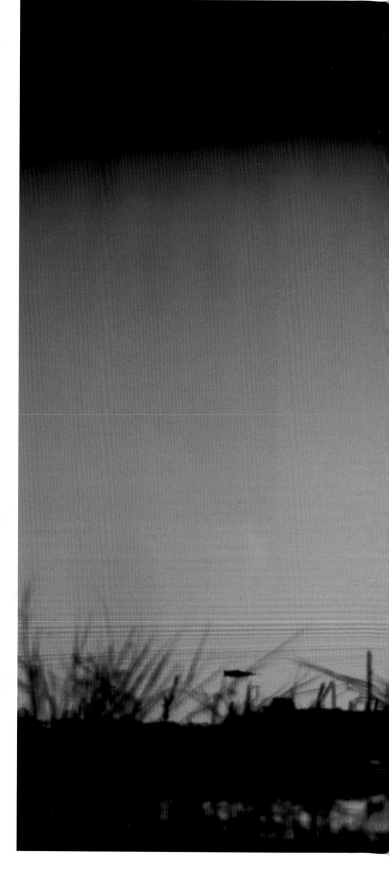

ELAWARE MUSEUM OF NATURAL HISTORY

Wild Delaware

THE PHOTOGRAPHY OF KEVIN FLEMING

Kevin Fleming began photographing Delaware's wildlife and wild places in August 2007. This exhibit records the natural resources of the Delaware River estuary, all of which can be seen within a 30-minute drive from where you are standing. To learn more about area wildlife, Kevin's photography, and his new book, *Wild Delaware* go to www.wilddelaware.com.

Presented by:
Delaware Museum of Natural History
4840 Kennett Pike, Wilmington, DE
302 658 9111   www.delmnh.org

Cape May - Lewes Ferry Terminal, Lewes, DE
June 5 – September 7, 2008
Delaware Museum of Natural History
November 1 – December 21, 2008

Sponsored by www.wilddelaware.com

Osprey (here and Preceding pages) • (Following pages) Harp Seal, Cape Henlopen State Park

PLANTS AND HABITAT:
the Foundation of Wild Delaware

William A. McAvoy

William A. McAvoy is a botanist with the Delaware Natural Heritage and Endangered Species Program in the Department of Natural Resources and Environmental Control.

When I consider the diversity of the natural world that makes Delaware "wild," I think first of the plants and their habitats that are native to the state and serve as the foundation on which Delaware's natural heritage is built. This

moon setting over deciduous trees

foundation is critical to the survival of our native wildlife species, as it provides them with food, cover and areas in which to breed.

Delaware is a small state, with about 1.3 million acres in its three counties. But this small geographic area hosts an impressive diversity of plant life — more than 1,500 documented species and varieties of native plants. This diversity stems from several factors: varied habitat types, a temperate climate and a geographic position within the eastern United States that places it

within a transition zone between the north and south.

Habitat is basically an area in which plants and animals reside; the dominant plants that grow within the area define the habitat. When discussing the state's diverse assortment of habitats, keep in mind that Delaware lies within two distinct physiographic provinces: the Piedmont and the Coastal Plain. The Piedmont is the hill country of northern New Castle County and comprises only 5 percent of the state; the flat Coastal Plain covers the rest. The two provinces have very different geological origins and ages, and thus have very different habitats and plant life.

Since Delaware is primarily Coastal Plain, where the nearly level landscape is conducive to the development of poorly drained soils, the state's most widespread habitat types are wetlands, both tidal and non-tidal. Tidal wetlands, which can be fresh, brackish or salt, develop along the streams, creeks and rivers that flow toward the coast and the Chesapeake Bay and appear as open marshes and swamps. Non-tidal wetlands also develop along streams and creeks, but can appear as isolated forested swamps or depressions. In the hill country of the Piedmont, wetlands are not as well developed as on the Coastal Plain, but non-tidal wetlands can still be found on the floodplains of streams and creeks, and at the base of steep wooded slopes.

On higher ground of both the Piedmont and Coastal Plain, where the soils are moist to well-drained, upland forests and woodland habitats develop. The canopy of these forests and woodlands are usually a mix of deciduous species, such as oaks (*Quercus* spp.), hickories (*Carya* spp.), beech (*Fagus grandifolia*) and tulip poplar (*Liriodendron tulipifera*). Evergreen species, such as loblolly pine (*Pinus taeda*) and Virginia pine (*P. virginiana*), often occur as well.

Delaware's temperate climate, moderated by the Delaware Bay, the Atlantic Ocean and the Chesapeake Bay, is one reason the state has a diverse collection of plant life. Our summers may at times be hot and humid but our winters are mild; precipitation is distributed fairly evenly throughout the year. Collectively, these conditions are all favorable to plant growth.

Delaware's plant diversity is influenced by its geographic position in the eastern United States, within a transition zone between the north and south. In other words, many species of plants that have their center of distribution north of Delaware are at or near their southern limits of distribution in the state; conversely, many plants that have their center of distribution south of the state are at or near their northern limits of distribution; 22 percent of the native plant life of Delaware has a more northern distribution, and 28 percent has a more southern distribution. Though our native plant life has a slightly more southern affinity, the meeting within the state of plants from both the north and south creates a diverse and interesting area of study.

From this basic understanding of Delaware's diverse plant life and habitats, we can discuss more specific themes. Let's begin in the Piedmont province, then work our way south onto the Coastal Plain, focusing on some of the more interesting habitat types and the unique plants they support.

In forests and on the steep woodland slopes of the Piedmont, where the soils are rich in organic matter and thus quite fertile, a habitat known as a "rich wood" develops and supports some of our most beautiful spring wildflowers, such as bloodroot (*Sanguinaria canadensis*), wild geranium (*Geranium maculatum*), round-lobed hepatica [*Anemone american* synonym = *Hepatica americana*)], yellow trout-lily (*Erythronium americanum*), showy orchis (*Galearis spectabilis*) and violet wood sorrel (*Oxalis violacea*). Ferns are well represented in this habitat and include species such as the maidenhair fern (*Adiantum pedatum*) and the broad-beech fern (*Phegopteris hexagonoptera*). Several state-rare and uncommon plants are found in this habitat: wild ginseng (*Panax*

quinquefolius), white baneberry (*Actaea pachypoda*) and the shrub eastern leatherwood (*Dirca palustris*).

As most of us have learned, species become rare primarily due to the loss and degradation of habitat, and over time Delaware has lost and degraded its share. Delaware was once mostly forested. Since the arrival of European settlers, the state has lost about 80 percent of its forest cover to agriculture and development. The forests that remain have been severely chopped up and fragmented; many exist as isolated islands in a sea of cropland or subdivisions. In

winter forest and moon setting

addition, thousands of acres of both tidal and non-tidal wetlands have been either filled or ditched to drain the land for the tilling of crops and the construction of houses and buildings. Such abuse of Delaware's natural heritage has taken a severe toll on our native plant life. Today, 36 percent (562 species) of the state's native plant life is considered rare, and 62 species are known from only a single location. In addition, 12 percent (180 species) of the state's native plant life is thought to be either historical (not seen for 20 or more years), or extirpated (gone from the state, never to be seen again).

first to become threatened by human-caused changes to their environments. Unfortunately, Delaware has no state laws or regulations that protect plants and their habitats, so if the destruction and degradation of habitat continues, many plants that are common today may become rare in the future.

Another Piedmont habitat that supports a unique suite of species are the floodplain wetlands found along some of the larger creeks in the province, such as the White Clay, Red Clay and the Brandywine. Some of the showier of these species that grow in the silty, nutrient-rich soils of the floodplains include Virginia bluebells (*Mertensia virginica*), Greek valerian (*Polemonium reptans*), eastern waterleaf (*Hydrophyllum virginianum*) and the green-headed coneflower (*Rudbeckia laciniata*). Some non-native invasive species severely threaten these characteristic plants of the floodplain wetlands. Most troublesome is the plant lesser celandine [*Ficaria verna* (synonym = *Ranunculus ficaria*)], which is so aggressive it can completely dominate an area of the floodplain to the exclusion of all native plants.

Non-native invasive plants can have a significant impact on our native plant life. Non-native plants are those that did not exist in North America before European settlement and are now well established in the natural landscape. Many of these plants arrived with the early settlers, either intentionally

White-tailed Deer and American Beech trees

Species rarity is not entirely due to the loss and degradation of habitat by humans; many species in Delaware are simply rare by their very nature and have always been rare in the state. Many state-rare species are very habitat-specific and require specialized environmental conditions; many are near the edge of their natural distribution and thus are infrequent to rare in their occurrence. However, these rare species that require specialized habitats, or those that are rare because they are edge-of-range species, are usually the

or unintentionally, or are modern-day garden escapes. To date, 674 species and varieties of non-native plants have been documented in Delaware. Non-native invasive plants are extremely aggressive in growth and have the ability to outcompete and displace our native vegetation. Non-native invasive species threaten the preservation of our native plant life, particularly plant species that are rare or uncommon. Considerable time and resources are expended trying to control the invaders; of those 674 non-native plant species, 87 are considered invasive.

The Piedmont's seepage slope wetland, a wetland that develops at the base of steep wooded slopes, where ground water seeps to the surface, is dominated by skunk cabbage (*Symplocarpus foetidus*) and the golden saxifrage (*Chrysosplenium americanum*). Other interesting plants occurring in this habitat include false hellebore (*Veratrum viride*), drooping sedge (*Carex prasina*), hooked buttercup (*Ranunculus recurvatus*), Pennsylvania bittercress (*Cardamine pensylvanica*), the state-rare rough sedge (*Carex scabrata*) and the log wood-fern (*Dryopteris celsa*).

Let us now head south on the Coastal Plain and discuss some of the habitats and plant life of this province. The flat Coastal Plain is conducive to the development of both tidal and non-tidal wetlands; the diversity of wetland types on the Coastal Plain is notable. One of the most abundant tidal wetland types is the salt marsh, which occurs along the Delaware Bay, the Atlantic Ocean and the Inland Bays of Sussex County. The principal plant that grows in salt marshes is the salt marsh cordgrass (*Spartina alterniflora*), and these marshes are often referred to as "spartina marshes." In the salt marsh, the dominant plants are grasses, sedges and rushes, including the big cordgrass (*S. cynosuroides*), salt hay (*S. patens*), salt marsh bulrush (*Schoenoplectus robustius*), three-square bulrush (*S. pungens*), needle rush (*Juncus roemarianus*) and black-grass rush (*J. gerardii*). Other plants that occur in the salt marsh include sea lavender (*Limonium carolinianum*), salt marsh fleabane (*Pluchea odorata*), seaside goldenrod (*Solidago sempervirens*) and the state-rare dwarf glasswort (*Salicornia bigelovii*). Unfortunately, thousands of acres of salt marshes throughout the state have been infested with the non-native grass, the common reed (*Phragmites australis* subsp. *australis*). This grass will form monocultures, or pure stands, which have very little value to wildlife and disrupt the complex ecological processes of the marsh. For many years much effort has been put towards controlling this species. Many gains have been made, but the species is so aggressive that we will likely be doing battle with it until the end of time.

While Delaware has many saltwater tidal marshes, sea-level rise, which may be the result of global warming, is making the occurrence of freshwater tidal marshes increasingly rare. Sea-level rise causes salt water from the bays and ocean to intrude farther up the tidal rivers and streams, making fresh water more salty; this will gradually change freshwater marshes to saltwater marshes. The species diversity within freshwater marshes is much higher than in salt marshes, and many of these plants are found only in freshwater tidal marsh habitat, so the loss of these marshes would be devastating to the wildlife that

Salt Marsh
Cordgrass

depend on them for survival. Freshwater tidal marshes occur infrequently within the estuary of the Delaware Bay; the state's most extensive acreage of freshwater tidal marsh habitat is found on the Nanticoke River. These marshes support a wide range of plant species, such as wild rice (*Zizania aquatica*), arrow-arum (*Peltandra virginica*), spatterdock (*Nuphar advena*), pickerelweed (*Pontederia cordata*), blue-flag iris (*Iris versicolor*), broad-leaf arrowhead (*Sagittaria latifolia*)

from taking up certain essential nutrients, Atlantic white cedar swamps are often home to carnivorous plants, which obtain the nutrients they are unable to get from the soil by digesting insects. Some of the state-rare carnivorous plants that primarily occur in Atlantic white cedar swamps include the purple pitcher plant (*Sarracenia purpurea*), round-leaf sundews (*Drosera rotundifolia*) and the humped bladderwort (*Utricularia gibba*). One of the most spectacular plants of Delaware's Atlantic white cedar swamps is the swamp pink (*Helonias bullata*). The swamp pink typically blooms in early spring; its wand-like cluster of bright pink flowers on a tall, leafless stem is quite striking. The swamp pink is state-rare; the U.S. Fish and Wildlife Service also lists it as threatened.

No discussion of swamps in Delaware would be complete without mention of the bald cypress swamp. Bald cypress (*Taxodium distichum*) is somewhat of a signature tree for Delaware, because it occurs at the extreme limit of its northern natural distribution. Most Delawareans are familiar with it, having seen it growing in Trap Pond State Park and nearby Trussum Pond. Most of our bald cypress swamps occur in south-

Cinnamon Fern and Crane Fly

and the state-rare riverbank sedge (*Carex lacustris*).

Atlantic white cedar swamps are an uncommon and fascinating wetland type that occurs in both tidal and non-tidal situations but they are most diverse in non-tidal habitats. Atlantic white cedar (*Chamaecyparis thyoides*), an extremely rot-resistant evergreen species, is the dominant tree of these swamps. The poorly drained soils in which it grows are extremely acidic. Because acidic soil conditions prevent most plants

central Sussex County, but three small ones are found farther north in Kent County; two are associated with the Murderkill River and the third, associated with the St. Jones River, is just south of Dover. Because bald cypress is at its northern limit in Delaware and only a few swamps remain, it is considered rare in the state.

Perhaps the most unique and important of Delaware's non-tidal wetland resources are Coastal Plain seasonal ponds, also known as Delmarva Bays or whale wallows. These are isolated, open, sunny depressions within forested areas. Usually smaller than one acre and often elliptical in shape, they are home to many state-rare plants and serve as critical breeding areas for salamanders, toads and frogs. Coastal Plain seasonal ponds are not permanent bodies of water; their water levels fluctuate with the seasons. In late winter and early spring the ponds are flooded when rain is plentiful and the groundwater table is high; by late summer and early fall the ponds are dry when rain is scarce and the groundwater table is low.

Coastal Plain seasonal ponds can be found in all three counties but are most frequently seen in the Blackbird region of southwestern New Castle County. State-rare plants found in Coastal Plain seasonal ponds include the awned meadow beauty (*Rhexia aristosa*), the pink tickseed sunflower (*Coreopsis rosea*) and the dwarf fimbry sedge (*Fimbristylis perpusilla*). One of the rarest grasses in the world, the Hirst's Brothers panic grass (*Dichanthelium hirstii*), is known in only six locations worldwide and one of them is in the Inland Bays region of Sussex County.

Fluctuating water levels drive the ecology of Coastal Plain seasonal ponds, and the plant and animal species found in these ponds depend on these fluctuating water levels to complete their life cycles. The featherfoil (*Hottonia inflata*) best describes this ecology. The featherfoil is an annual species and its seeds germinate in the ponds when they are dry in late summer and early fall. After germination, a small rosette of leaves develops and will overwinter in standing water. In early spring, when the ponds are flooded, a long stem forms from the rosette and grows toward the water surface. From

Swamp Pink

this stem, new hollow stems develop, allowing the plant to float on the water's surface while flowering and setting seed. Once the seed matures, it drops and floats to the bottom of the pond where it waits for the pond to dry, starting the process all over again.

Delaware's non-tidal fresh water wetlands support the highest diversity of rare plants in the state, but these habitats have very limited and, in most cases, no federal, state or county protection. Should we lose these wetlands, or allow them to continue to degrade, future generations will question why we did not do more to protect and preserve this important part of our natural heritage.

With so many habitats and even more intriguing plants, our state offers countless opportunities for outdoor exploration. I do hope this summary encourages you to learn more and inspires you to actually explore the wilds of Delaware.

Canada geese

"If... we can live without goose music, we may as well do away with stars, or sunsets..."

–Aldo Leopold

Canada goose gosling

Skunk kit

Opossum joey

Red Fox kit

"The last word in
ignorance is the
man who says of
an animal or plant:
what good is it?
...To keep every
cog and wheel is
the first precaution
of intelligent
tinkering."

–Aldo Leopold

Black Vulture chicks in abandoned farm silo • (Following pages) Groundhog

(Left) Red Fox • Gray Fox kit • (Following pages) Red Fox

(Left) Savannah Sparrow • Red-winged Blackbird • (Preceding pages) Fowler Beach sunrise

THE GREAT MARSH

Jennifer Ackerman
Award-winning science writer Jennifer Ackerman is the author of three books, *Notes from the Shore; Chance in the House of Fate: A Natural History of Heredity,* and, most recently, *Sex Sleep Eat Drink Dream: A Day in the Life of Your Body.* She writes for **National Geographic**, **The New York Times** and other publications.

The Great Marsh is a broad plain of mud and grass that lies a mile northwest of Lewes. It's roughly rectangular, five square miles, bordered on three sides by uplands and on the fourth, by Beach Plum Island. Along the southern border Oyster Rocks Neck and Hells Neck run a half mile or so into the marsh, their wooded uplands reaching an elevation of about ten feet. A few islands, or hummocks, rise out of the sea of grass and support little forests of pine and cedar, sassafras, red maple and black gum. Otherwise, this is a landscape of no relief, flat and featureless. The major tool for navigating here is the system of tortuous streams that crease the grassy plain: Canary Creek, Fisher Creek, Black Hog Gut, and Old Mill Creek, which meanders in giant loopy S-curves from Red Mill Pond to the Broadkill River and drains nearly three-quarters of the marsh. The Delaware Bay flows dendritically through Old Mill Creek and its tributaries. The creeks predate the marsh, which was born 7,000 years ago when the rapidly rising sea drowned a valley of the Broadkill River, transforming it into a small lagoon. Silt gradually clogged the lagoon and filled it; then pioneering grasses advanced over the mud, trapping soil in the tiny baffles of their roots and anchoring it to make marsh.

The Great Marsh and Canary Creek

JUST BEFORE SUNRISE, LOW TIDE. I walk out into the marsh in the dark, stepping around chocolate-brown pools agitated with the scratching and scuttling of fiddler crabs, past delicate marsh pinks, absent their color in the white-wash light. Waves of warm air waft up from the mudbanks bared by the outcreeping tide, a strong sulfur smell, not unpleasant. The beam of my flashlight catches the giant ghostly pale blossoms of the seashore mallow, *Kosteletzkya virginica*. I linger here for a moment, hoping to "shine" the eyes of a wolf spider, a species with mirror-like membranes that reflect light. The darkness of the marsh is not the close darkness of woods, where blackness pours up

long pants and a flannel shirt. Beneath the grass is a deep black brew of rivers silt and clay trapped over millennia, bottomed twenty feet down by hard-packed yellow sand. Every fifteen steps or so I sink deep in a soft oozy hole. When I reach the tower, I peel off my damp shirt and my hipwaders, coated with a glossy mud sheen, and sit in my socks.

The sky above the Great Marsh is so broad that it hosts more than one celestial event. This morning a sagging August moon a day or two past full is setting in the west, and in the east, a tomato of a sun is edging up over the horizon. Soon it's swallowed up by a reef of purple clouds, casting the marsh in monochromatic

light. The tower's open, rickety crow's-nest platform offers a 360-degree view of the low country around it. I can just make out the lean profile of a great blue heron well camouflaged by stillness. It plunges its head into a pool and comes up with a fish, swallows it and then raises itself slowly with deep parenthetical beats of its huge wings. I can hear the cackle of a green heron, but can't pick it out of the ranks of green roughage.

For months after I arrived here, I did not understand the draw of this leveled, subdued landscape, couldn't focus on any one part of it long enough to penetrate its surface. Then one summer I spent time in the tower with a young scientist from the Delaware Division

Great Blue Heron and Mantis Shrimp

from between the trees, but a thin, liquid, open, far-reaching darkness that descends onto the grass. Silence stretches from horizon to horizon, broken only by the occasional call of a whippoorwill, a sound that carries easily over the flat topography, somehow amplified by the open acres of air and the drum-flat surface of the nearby bay.

My destination is a small tower of metal scaffolding fifteen feet high topped by a wooden blind that sits about a mile into the marsh. The path to the tower is wandering and uncertain and moves erratically between firm ground and sloppy bottom that sucks hungrily at my hipwaders. Even in the night damp I'm sweating profusely, bundled against mosquitoes in

of Fish and Wildlife. Randy Cole is a native of this place who was raised on duck hunting and wears his hipwaders like a second skin. He is studying the wildlife drawn to several artificial ponds dug into the marsh a few seasons before. The ponds are part of a state program designed to control mosquitoes and at the same time, draw back some of the wildlife that has been chivied out by earlier mosquito-control efforts.

In the 1930s state officials had a complex system of crisscrossing ditches cut into the marsh, not with the loops and curves of natural creeks, but with the straight lines and right angles of the planning grid. In so doing they broke the natural order of the marsh, disturbed a rhythm old and of vast importance. The grid-ditching drained the big natural ponds whose permanent waters once attracted breeding colonies of black ducks and gadwall. The new ponds, a dozen half-acre pools contoured for natural effect, are designed to bring the birds back.

Randy's job is to record the species and number of animals that use the ponds for feeding or breeding. While we sit and watch for waterfowl, he points out salient marsh plants: *Spartina alterniflora*, or smooth cordgrass; saltmeadow hay; sea lavender; spike grass; and *Salicornia*, or saltwort. The latter is an odd little thing with leaves like long swollen toes, the only plant that can survive the extreme salinity found in the salt pans that pockmark the higher marsh, where water has been concentrated by evaporation until its salt content is several times that of the sea. At this time of year its spears are turning red from the roots up, giving it the look of a bizarre Christmas ornament made of flesh.

The marsh vegetation was to my first bewildered surveys utterly indistinct. Over time, however, it has slowly sorted itself into recognizable zones, not altogether different from a mountain's, where leafy deciduous woodland gives way to pines, and then to treeless tundra — only here the distinction between zones comes down to shifts in inches.

In the marsh's higher reaches — the hummocks and along the landward edges, out of reach of all but the highest spring or storm tides — grow two woody plants collectively called saltbush. There's marsh elder, *Iva frutescens*, an awkward stalky shrub with thick, fleshy leaves, and *Baccharis halimifolia*, the groundsel tree. Now in late summer, its seedheads look like hundreds of tiny white plumes. Below, but still wetted only twice a month by spring tides, grows salt-meadow hay, windrows of fine light stalks that swirl and mat in giant cowlicks. Lower still, by only two inches or so, salt-meadow hay gives way to the big, coarse, dark green stalks of *Spartina alterniflora*, which are flooded by every tide. *Spartina* is remarkable for its rich ability to solicit sunlight and its ingenious adaptations to the

salt flood that sweeps through the marsh twice daily. Close to a million cubic feet of brackish water flow in during flood tide, nearly doubling the water's salt content. Salt sucks water from living cells. But by special cunning *Spartina* can drink the water while excluding the salt: membranes on the plant's roots pull the freshwater from the sea. What little salt makes its way into the sap is excreted by glands in the plant's leaves. At low tide you can see the exiled salt crystals flashing in the sun.

On the walk out to the tower, Randy would squat down to show me the miniature tropical forest amid the thick stems of *Spartina*, a hot, humid,

nearly windless environment. On and around the stems grows a microscopic, polycultural jungle of hundreds of species of diatoms, algae and dinoflagellates, which trap phosphorus, nitrates and other elements vital to marsh life. Beneath it all, the marsh mud is black, blacker than the soil of the Mississippi Delta, and richer. Each autumn the aerial stems of *Spartina* die, bend down, break and mix into the black muck. Bacteria decompose the leaves, breaking them into small particles, detritus, which the tide spreads across the marsh surface, providing a pasture of food. An astronomer friend of mine saw this instantly when he looked down on the mud: "This place is *trashed* with life."

moonrise over Canary Creek

Pull up the blanket of marsh, give it a shake, and out would tumble coffee-bean snails, *Melampus bidentatus*, little half-inch creatures tinted with brown and green, as well as grasshoppers, beetles, ants, flies, and cinch bugs, which feed on *Spartina*'s tender leaves, and plant hoppers, which suck its juices. Also fiddler crabs and mud crabs, oysters and dense clumps of ribbed mussels, which pave the mud along the creeks where the tide floods regularly. According to one study, this marsh supports more than three and a half million mussels per acre. Out, too, would tumble diamondback terrapins, turtles the size of a small skull, their segmented

American Bumble Bee on Crimson-Eyed Rosemallow

pentagons fused to form a leathery dome; their reptilian heads spotted like a leopard. The diamondback was once here in great numbers, but its sweet flesh made it a gastronomic delicacy and the target of tireless collectors.

The shake wouldn't loose such tenacious insiders as the larva of the common marsh fly, family *Chloropidae*, which lives in the stems of *Spartina* and eats the plant's tissue. (The adults are so small, only two or three millimeters long, that they are nearly invisible except when swarming.) Nor would it dislodge the larvae of the fierce-biting greenhead fly, whose singular appetites are described by John and Mildred Teal in *Life and*

Death of the Salt Marsh. "The larvae are maggots, soft, elongate, leathery-skinned, lumpy individuals with a pair of organs for breathing air at one end and a pair of sharp jaws at the other. They wriggle through the mud eating anything they come across, including others of their kind. If a number of *Tabanus* maggots are put together in a dish, the end result is one fat, temporarily contented individual."

Here are some of the thirty or so species of fish that swim the waters of the Great Marsh: the small, glistening fish known as silversides, the four-spined stickleback, anchovy, northern pipefish, two kinds of herring, young striped bass, sea robins, summer flounder, naked gobies, striped mullet and white perch, eel, croaker, menhaden, northern kingfish, and three species of killifish, including the mummichog, a name that comes from a Narragansett word meaning "they go in great numbers."

The sun has reappeared above the cloud reef, a second bloom. In this low morning light the marsh looks different than it does under cloud cover or high sun; not a hazy watercolor wash, but a dazzling mosaic of distinctly different greens. The tide is sliding up the marsh slope, slithering into the creeks and spilling over between the blades of grass. The up, down, in, out of the tides makes this place dangerous — sometimes inundating animals with lethal doses of saltwater, sometimes exposing them to a devastating high-and-dry death — but also inconceivably rich. The tides distribute food and flush out waste, encouraging rapid growth and quick decay. Adaptation to this pulse is the contract that all successful marsh creatures have signed with a country half land, half sea. When the ebbing tide bares the flats, hundreds of scraping chitinous legs and claws scribe the mud as fiddler crabs emerge from their burrows to search for bacteria, fungi, minute algae and fermenting marsh plants.

Tiny star-shaped pigment cells dotting the crab's body obey the compounded rhythms of sun and tide. The cells contain granules of dark pigment, which disperse at daytime low tide, giving the crabs the color of the mudbank and thus protecting them from predators. At night the pigment granules shrink from the cell's reaches and cluster together, the color fades, and the crabs turn the pale ivory-white of moonlight. These changes occur every day at a different hour, synchronized with the tides.

Now, as the salt tide seeps up the mudbank, the fiddlers are waiting until the water reaches their knees before they disappear into their deep mud tunnels to wait out the deluge. Though they breathe air with a primitive lung beneath the edge of their shell, they can hole up in their burrows with no oxygen for long periods — for months in cold water — a feat that makes the limit of our own tolerance for organic variation seem narrow indeed. A few moments' loss of oxygen and we rapidly descend into unconsciousness.

Coffee-bean snails, too, are air-breathers, but they go up rather than down when the tide rises. Like ghost crabs and beach fleas, they are members of a race that is learning to live outside the sea. Somehow they anticipate rising tides, creeping up the stalks of grass well before the water arrives. They take a breath of air that will hold them for an hour or so if the drowning sea submerges them.

Spiders and insects such as grasshoppers keep company with the snail, scaling stems to escape the high tide. This habit exposes the climbers to the keen eyes and hungry beaks of birds. The Teals once described the scene of an especially high tide, insects hopping, jumping, and flying onto taller plants until "only the tallest grasses along the creeks mark the meandering channels and these grasses are weighted and bending at the tips, alive with insects. Sparrows and wrens from the marsh, buntings and warblers from the land, gulls and terns from the beach, and swallows, dip, fly, settle and swim along the twisting lanes of helpless insects and gorge themselves."

I've seen swallows swooping over the marsh, snatching insects in midair, then suddenly dodging a marsh hawk's hook and talon in a startling turnabout of predator and prey.

Sunlight to marsh grass to grasshopper to swallow to hawk: these are some of the links that compose the marsh web. Learning a place is like this, glimpsing the individuals, the pinpoint touches of color on the broad canvas, randomly splattered. You pick them out, sort them out, name them, then tumble them back into the landscape, and by reading and more observation, figure out how they fit together. As more spaces are filled in, the image or weave is revealed, the continuous meshing intimacy. It helps to have a native tutor, and a sense of the storyline, the narrative over time. In the marsh, the little rhythms of the day have a way of focusing attention on particular species, the way the slow, small meter of an Emily Dickinson poem brings each syllable into close-up.

Greenhead Fly

NOON, HIGH TIDE. The marsh is a flat, dazzling mirror anchored by green studs. The high sun has robbed it of the play of shifting light in which it luxuriated this morning, brought it silently to whiteness. It looks uninhabited, and yet I know that each square inch of mud is crowded with twitchers, alive with drama, tragedy, plot and adventure, fierce eating and being eaten.

The mosquitoes have left me alone this morning, but once the sun goes down, I'll hear what D. H. Lawrence called that "small, high, hateful bugle in my ear." Huge swarms of mosquitoes used to range over this region, bands of million moving in unison, several feet thick and hundreds of feet wide, their frenzied wingbeats producing a single, singing hum. In 1788 an observer at Cape Henlopen wrote:

The people are afflicted with a eveil, not much unlike, and almost as severe as, some of the plagues of Egypt. I mean the inconceivable swarms of muscatoes and sandflies which infest every place, and equally interrupt the tranquility of the night and the happiness of the day. Their attacks are intolerable upon man as well as beast. The poor cows and horses in order to escape from these tormentors stand whole days in ponds of water with only their heads exposed.

of the pool, breathing through little snorkel-like air tubes and feeding on microscopic organisms. On their way to adulthood, they pass through four larval stages and a pupal phase, a metamorphosis that in warm weather can take less than ten days. When the adults emerge, they mate over the marsh. Then the females set out to search for a blood meal.

In the early 1930s a man could make a dollar a day digging ditches for the Delaware Mosquito Control Commission. The answer to the problem of the salt-marsh mosquito, the state believed, lay in disrupting the insect's life cycle by draining off the small shallow ponds of water that served as breeding pools. With this in mind, managers placed a grid of dots over maps of Delaware's marshes and then connected the dots with a ruler. These straight lines would become ditches hand-dug, twenty inches wide, twenty inches deep, one hundred fifty feet apart, which would drain all marshes, high and low, whether or not they were suitable breeding grounds for mosquitoes.

To help with the project, the federal government assigned four companies from the Civilian Conservation Corps, eight hundred men. One company set up camp in Lewes in a big building on Savannah Road topped by a brass and copper weathervane in the shape of a giant mosquito.

The ditch digging was slow, hard work, but the operation was conducted with military efficiency. In four years the Corps had installed 11.5 million linear feet of ditches across 44,000 acres of Delaware, including virtually all of the salt marsh in the southeastern part of the state.

Diamondback Terrapin

Delaware is home to fifty-three species of mosquitoes — with names like *Aedes excrucians, Coquilletiddia perturbans, A. tormentor,* and *A. vexans* — each adapted to occupy a particular niche. The high marsh saltmeadow hay around her suits *A. sollicitans,* the salt-marsh mosquito. Females of the species lay their eggs in the moist mud of potholes found in and around the tufts of salt hay, which are flooded only infrequently. When spring tides or storm tides or rainfall fill the potholes, the eggs quickly hatch. The larvae rest just under the surface

Every time they dug one of those ditches, it was like pulling the plug from a bathtub. The full effects are only now being uncovered. The rookeries of breeding waterfowl and other birds have shrunk or disappeared for want of pools in which to feed. Where the ditching changed water levels, that tall, tassel-fringed reed, *Phragmites australis,* spread across the marsh, crowding out the marsh grasses so essential to the food web. In some places, the drainage ditches opened areas of marsh to more frequent flooding at

Sand Fiddler Crab

lower tide levels. Less organic debris accumulated on marsh surfaces and populations of invertebrates at the base of the marsh food web crashed. Ironically, the small pools that formed behind the mounds of spoil created new breeding grounds for *A. sollicitans.*

The orderly ousting of the low, wet lands along this coast is not a new thing. For hundreds of years, people have considered these worlds miasmic, breeding grounds of choking vapors, of "exhalations [that] produced ague and intermittent fevers in the autumn and plursies in the spring," said an 1838 edition of the *Delaware Register and Farmers' Magazine*. The only good marsh was a drained marsh. Beginning in the 17th century, the Dutch — those masters of land

Green Heron

drainage in Europe — and their colonial successors ditched and diked the miry edges of the New World to create farmland and the squared geometry of our coastal towns. In the 1780s Delaware had 480,000 acres of marshes and swamps. In the 1990s only half of that remained.

Late afternoon pivots into dusk. The tide has begun to recede without my noticing, the eddying currents carrying out the rich detritus from decayed *Spartina* that will feed the hordes of tiny planktonic animals that are themselves food for the greater creatures of the bay and sea.

One proposed solution to the destruction of wetlands is mitigation or "no net loss." The idea is this:

Anyone who destroys a wetland must create one of similar size somewhere else. Plant some grass, introduce some keystone species, and hope that these serve as a sort of gravitational force that will draw in the myriad elements of the marsh community. But no new marsh can re-create the complex chemistry of mud cooked over millennia, the dying down of *Spartina* in the cool of a thousand autumns, the slow, steady mixing of bacteria and algae. Nor can it guarantee the proper assembly of species, birds, insects, plants, bacteria, each occupying a precise niche and locked in intimate relationships. The created marsh may look like a marsh to the casual eye, the eye of the passer-by. Perhaps in some measure it acts like one. But it is not the real thing. Is it enough to make replicas, perfectly intelligible and diminished?

SUNSET, LOW TIDE. The mosquitoes have finally found me, tipped off by the hot chemical breath of my skin. They are odd sorts of carnivores. "The lady whines, then dines; is slapped and killed," says poet Brad Leithauser, "yet it's her killer's blood that has been spilled."

It's true that only the female pursues a blood meal: the male sticks to nectar. Only she has the long stabbing mouthparts that penetrate skin. These form a flexible tube with serrations that neatly slice my skin tissue and a curved tip that scans for blood just beneath the skin's surface. When the mosquito finds a capillary, she draws the blood up through the tube with two sturdy pumps in her head. At the same time, she sends saliva back down another hollow tube. The saliva, which inhibits the clotting of blood, causes the irritating itching and swelling. It can also carry disease. When Thomas Nuttall traveled across the country almost two hundred years ago, he took with him a one-celled parasite of the genus *Plasmodium*, which he had picked up from an *Anopheles* mosquito he met in a Delaware swamp. During most of his remaining years, he suffered attacks of malaria.

Those wading birds on the ponds below are my partners in torment. Mosquitoes find their bills and eyes, the flesh peeking through their thin head feathers, their long exposed legs. A hunting green heron will let biting mosquitoes cover its legs and head before it will twitch or flutter and lose its prey.

Our blood provides the female mosquito with the protein she needs to produce a new generation. She'll suck up to four times her own weight at a single sitting, about a millionth of a gallon, which she stores in her inner abdomen. (A two-bit tour of the insect would have to pause at this organ, unfettered by appendages and therefore able to distend enormously to house blood.) Her swelling gut triggers the secretion of hormones that prompt her eggs to mature. One blood meal provides enough nutrition to produce up to two hundred eggs. Without it, she can lay only a dozen eggs or so.

You have to admire the power packed into her thrumming body. One ten-thousandth of an ounce and a brain only slightly bigger than the period at the end of this sentence. Her wings hum at two hundred to five hundred beats per second and will carry her up to fifty miles from her brood marsh in search of a blood meal. She can lay a new batch of eggs every two weeks, and may lay as many as three or four batches of eggs during her summer of existence.

Aldo Leopold says that the beauty of marshes doesn't scream at you; it has a slow, lyrical welling effect. Likewise, the deterioration beneath its green ranks only gradually discloses itself, and only to the knowing eye.

One woman here knows the marsh well, sees it intimately like the house of her childhood, now skewed and malfunctioning, with termite-eaten floorboards, frayed wiring, rotting beams. She fights hard to save it, with some success: Her detractors call her the wicked witch of the wetlands. I've seen her at meetings with officials deciding the fate of one piece of drowned country after another. She knits while she listens, her needles flashing and clicking harder and faster as her rage mounts, and I wonder whether those pale pink sweaters and booties don't contain the names of the bureaucrats and businessmen who would do in our marshlands.

Randy Cole sees it, too, sees the body with skin intact but bones broken. Gone are the great pools of open water that once covered forty acres of the Great Marsh,

pools that were nearly always full, replenished twice in twenty-four hours by tidal streams from the great sea, twice left brimming for crowds of rummaging, raucous ducks, their wings striking water again and again before they broke into the air. In recent seasons, Randy has found few breeding birds; the artificial ponds are not working the open water sorcery.

The plaster falls from a mural; locusts consume a section of tapestry, taking with it some critical incidents. Consider the elements of any tale: Pull one out and the story changes. If John Donne is right, any death diminishes the whole, even the death of an obscure piece of damp ground. It is, in its way, a reservoir of old authority and a link to our own beginnings.

Snow Goose feather on Salt Wort

I swat as evening descends. In the low light there is a kind of intense clarity, a last assertion of detail. Then the light withdraws slowly, and the detail weakens, evaporates, bleeds away. The lines of grass dissolve; the hummocks lose their outline, then their form, gradually, almost imperceptibly. There is a graying, a blending, as everything becomes dim, incomprehensible. The first star is out, a white diamond in a sea of night sky.

The Great Marsh essay first appeared in *Notes from the Shore* (Viking Penguin, 1995).

(Following pages) rainbow over Canary Creek

Surviving for more than 250 million years - eons before the dinosaurs became extinct - Horseshoe Crabs (preceding pages) are facing new threats to their existence from harvesting and habitat destruction. So too are the many species of migratory birds and sea creatures that depend on the Horseshoe Crab. Every spring tens of thousands of Horseshoe Crabs mate and lay millions of pinhead-sized eggs along the Delaware Bay beaches from Lewes to Woodland Beach. And thousands of migratory shorebirds like

the Red Knot (above) gather along the shore to feast on the protein-rich eggs.

Red Knots make one of the longest migrations of any bird traveling more than 9,000 miles from Tierra del Fuego in southern South America to its Canadian Arctic breeding grounds. In May, they concentrate along the Delaware Bay in numbers that may be as high as 90% of the entire Red Knot subspecies (*Calidris canutus rufa*) population.

Willet, Ruddy Turnstones,
Semipalmated Sandpipers and Red Knot
(Preceding pages) Horseshoe Crabs mating

Ruddy Turnstones   •   (Preceding pages) Semipalmated Sandpiper

Killdeer

DELAWARE'S AMPHIBIANS AND REPTILES

Jim White

Jim White is a native Delawarean, with more than 30 years of experience studying and teaching about the state's amphibians and reptiles. He is co-author, with his wife Amy, of Amphibians and Reptiles of Delmarva, a 250-page field guide to the 70 amphibian and reptile species known to occur on the Delmarva Peninsula. He is currently associate director for land and biodiversity management at the Delaware Nature Society.

It's a rainy night, mild for January, when most Delawareans are nestled in a warm house, sipping a hot beverage and enjoying a good movie or book. Unlike these sensible folk, I'm decked out in chest waders and raincoat, standing waist-deep in 40-degree water, somewhere in the wilds of Delaware. The amphibian and reptile year has begun.

With a bright flashlight I scan downward through the tea-colored water, searching for the first "herps" (short for herptiles — amphibians and reptiles) of the year. If I've chosen the right night, I'll soon spot my first amphibian swimming lazily along the bottom — an adult Eastern Tiger Salamander. This rare and, at up to nearly 8 inches long, Delaware's largest salamander has a dark body with dull yellow blotches creating a camouflage that makes it barely observable in the dark water. This individual and others of his species have come to reproduce in the cold, murky waters of this vernal pool, a seasonally-flooded depression that typically fills with water during winter or spring and dries by late summer or early fall.

If I'm really lucky — I've only seen this once in about 100 visits — I could even get to observe the species' secretive mating ritual. It goes something like this: The male performs an underwater courtship "dance" that includes aggressive nudging and tail-wagging. If the female appears interested, the male deposits a packet of sperm on leaves or sticks on the bottom of the pool. The male leads the female overtop the sperm packet so that she can pick it up with her cloacal lips and insert it into her cloaca, thus fertilizing her eggs internally. Soon after, the female attaches several gelatinous egg masses to submerged twigs. After completing mating and egg-laying, both males and females exit the pool, crawling silently back to the surrounding woodlands, where they burrow underground and leave the next generation to develop on their own. I'll have to revisit the pool in a month or so if I want to observe the newly hatched, gilled larvae as they swim about feeding on aquatic invertebrates and other amphibian larvae.

On the long drive home I think about the herp year ahead of me — how, when, and where I will be able to observe some of the 27 species of amphibians (salamanders and frogs) and 39 species of reptiles (turtles, lizards and snakes) that live in Delaware. We're fortunate that the state's mild climate and abundance of wetlands provide habitats and conditions favorable for such a diversity of herps. Finding and observing them in the wild, however, can be challenging, as most species are small and secretive.

Although the herp year starts off slowly, with only a few species active in the cold of winter, by the time spring arrives, Delaware's wild lands will come alive with a flurry of breeding activity.

Eastern Hog-nosed Snake

February is still a cold month in Delaware; however, every once in a while winter loosens its grip and there are days that hint of spring. On these unusually mild days, several of Delaware's frog species emerge from their hibernation in the mud. Adult male frogs call loudly from wetlands, producing species-specific mating calls to attract females. The first calls I usually hear are the dry, ascending trills of the New Jersey Chorus Frog and the very loud, high-pitched peeps of the Spring Peeper. These small tree frogs are difficult to

Eastern Tiger
Salamander

manifestations of some deep-seated fears that remain from times when humans lived in closer contact with the natural world or are a result of myths and media hype that have been passed down from generation to generation, the result is the same: most humans do not like snakes. Nevertheless, humans are also almost universally interested in these fascinating animals. In Delaware, the harmless Common Watersnake, Eastern Gartersnake and Common Ribbonsnake are often the first snakes found warming in the spring sunshine or searching for frogs and other prey along the edge of wetlands.

The small but very handsome Spotted Turtle is also most active in the spring, often basking on logs, banks and debris, especially on sunny spring mornings. As its name implies, this turtle has bright yellow or orange spots on its black carapace (top shell). It is rarely seen during the hot, dry summer months, and it is possible that it aestivates (sort of a summer hibernating) during this period. Although this species is fairly common in some parts of Delaware, overall populations appear to be declining, largely due to habitat loss, as many of the wetland areas in which Spotted Turtles live have been destroyed. Also, the Spotted Turtle is popular in the pet trade

see, hidden in the wetlands, but they are easy to hear as they call loudly. Another early season frog is the Wood Frog. The males and females of this otherwise terrestrial species make their way to the breeding pools for a frenzied but relatively short-lived breeding season in February or March. The abrupt clucking calls of male Wood Frogs can be heard emanating from vernal, woodland pools throughout the state.

As the days lengthen, the warming sun encourages the first snakes to emerge from their hibernation. More than any other vertebrate group, snakes instill fear and disgust in many humans. Whether these emotions are

and is susceptible to over-collecting.

At the first hint of the approaching summer, several other herp species become active. Our largest and one of our most common snakes, the Eastern Ratsnake, can often be seen scaling the trunk of a tree searching for some of its favorite prey: bird eggs and nestlings. The tables are often turned, however, as hawks, herons and other large birds, as well as several carnivorous animals, prey upon the snakes. Snakes are even fed upon by other snakes. For example, the Eastern Kingsnake feeds aggressively on other snakes and even eats snakes nearly its own size, including the venomous

Copperhead. Like many of Delaware's snakes, Kingsnakes can be found by turning over boards and other debris. When threatened, a Kingsnake may coil, vibrate its tail and even strike. Like many other snakes, it discharges a foul-smelling musk from its anal glands when first handled.

In late spring several more frog species begin to breed, their calls creating a cacophony emanating from the state's freshwater wetlands. The welcome warm days and nights are the stimulus for the Gray Treefrog, Cope's Gray Treefrog, Eastern Cricket Frog, Green Treefrog and others to begin calling at vernal pools on the Coastal Plain.

Delaware's rarest and most spectacular frog — the Barking Treefrog — breeds in late spring and early summer. This plump, bright green species, found primarily in the southeast, is the largest tree frog native to the United States. It was long thought to occur only as far north as Norfolk, Virginia, but in 1984 I discovered a population in southern New Castle County, and I've since found other populations in Sussex County and in nearby Maryland. Male Barking Treefrogs call from the surface of vernal pools and borrow pits and their very loud, hound-like barking can be heard almost a mile away. As with most other Delaware tree frogs, after the breeding season the adults spend the warm months in trees and shrubs.

In summer Delawareans head to the coast, and that's where you want to be if you're looking for the Northern Diamondback Terrapin. It is the only turtle in Delaware — and one of a few kinds in the world — that lives exclusively in brackish to saltwater habitats. I've seen hundreds of terrapins in May and June swimming just off the sandy beaches of the Delaware Bay. It's impressive to see them basking on the mudflats at low tide, sometimes on the backs of horseshoe crabs.

The terrapin uses its extremely strong jaws and hard "beak" to feed on a variety of hard-shelled estuarine invertebrates, including fiddler and hermit crabs, mud snails, periwinkles, mussels, clams and other small mollusks. In spring it also eats horseshoe crab eggs by the thousands. In June and July, nesting females crawl from the water to search for suitable nesting sites above the high tide. Unfortunately, many female terrapins are killed as they crawl across roads, moving to and from favored nesting sites.

Spotted Turtle

Summertime at our southern beaches, particularly in the scrubby sand dunes, provides the right time and place to observe one of only four lizards that occur in Delaware, the Eastern Fence Lizard. This small brown lizard avoids deep woods, preferring areas with abundant sunlight on the edges of woods and fields. It is especially common around logs, woodpiles, stone piles, other human-deposited debris and buildings (as well as on fences) in the southern part of the state. When threatened, it typically climbs the nearest tree or other vertical structure and hides on the far side, similar to the behavior seen in gray squirrels.

Another reptile that favors sandy habitats is the Eastern Hog-nosed Snake. It is named for its upturned, shovel-like snout, which it uses to probe the soil for its primary prey — the Fowler's Toad. When disturbed by a predator or curious human, this snake, the drama queen (or king) of the herpetological world, usually responds with bluffing behavior. It puffs up with air, widens its head and neck and raises its head in cobra-like fashion while emitting a loud hissing sound. If this

peninsula: the Northern Green Frog and the American Bullfrog. The green frog's explosive breeding call, reminiscent of the sound produced by plucking a loose banjo string, and the deep "jug-o-rum" sound of the bullfrog are among Delaware's most familiar summer nature sounds. Both species lay their eggs in raft-like sheets on the surface of the water and both have a relatively long tadpole stage — up to one year for green frogs and up to two years for bullfrogs.

As the dog days of summer progress, finding herps becomes more difficult. Most species cannot tolerate the hot, dry summer, so they either become predominantly nocturnal or move to cool, moist, sometimes underground, retreats. However, late summer is still a good time to see many of Delaware's turtles. A trip to a local pond will often produce observations of the Eastern Painted Turtle, Eastern Musk Turtle and the monstrous Eastern Snapping Turtle, either swimming just below the water's surface or basking in the sun on logs or banks. One of the largest and most conspicuous of the basking turtles is the Northern Red-bellied Cooter. It can easily be observed sunning on stumps and logs in any of the state's many millponds.

Northern
Green Frog

tactic doesn't scare the intruder away, the snake typically feigns death by writhing rapidly, turning over on its back, opening its mouth, extending its tongue, and sometimes even regurgitating its last meal before finally lying still. If picked up, the snake feels flaccid, as if the body has started to decay. However, if the snake is placed back on the ground right-side up, it will again turn over onto its back, revealing that it is indeed still alive.

Anyone who has visited a pond during the summer has surely heard two of the most common frogs on the

One of the best places to observe turtles at close range is at Silver Lake in Rehoboth Beach. Apparently the turtles have become habituated to being fed and hang around the footbridge at the upper end of the lake. Here you can see the Red-eared Slider, a non-native species originally from the south-central United States. In the 1950s and 1960s, thousands of young sliders were sold to America's youth as pets, complete with small plastic tubs and palm trees. Although most probably died in captivity, others survived and were released into local ponds. Over the years these turtles have thrived in many of our millponds.

As the cool of autumn descends, many amphibians and reptiles become less active and prepare to begin hibernation. The cool nights and warm days do, however, offer opportunities to observe several snake species. For example, the bright and slender Northern Rough Greensnake can be found entwined in the branches of shrubs and other vegetation along the edges of wetlands. This graceful, tropical-looking snake hunts for insects such as dragonflies and grasshoppers. It is easily overlooked because its long, slender, green body blends perfectly with green leaves, twigs and vines (particularly greenbrier). When handled, the northern Rough Green Snake may display defensively by opening its mouth to show off its purple-black interior, but it rarely attempts to bite.

Although Delaware's one venomous snake, the Copperhead, can be observed in spring and summer, fall seems to produce the most observations. To say that the vast majority of Delawareans will never see a Copperhead is an understatement. This is partly because in Delaware they live only in isolated populations in the vicinity of Alapocas Woods in northern New Castle County and in the southern half of Sussex County. However, each year I receive many calls from people mistakenly reporting sightings. Usually the snake in question turns out to be a Common Watersnake, Eastern Hog-nosed Snake or juvenile Eastern Ratsnake. It may be hard to believe, but the Copperhead is relatively docile and reluctant to strike unless stepped on or otherwise provoked. Cases of humans being bitten in Delaware are very rare. In recent times, no deaths directly attributable to Copperhead bites have been reported in Delaware. Nevertheless, this snake should never be handled, and caution should be taken when in Copperhead habitat because the bite, though rarely fatal, is still dangerous, particularly for young children and the elderly. Adult Copperheads feed mainly on small mammals and birds, while juveniles feed mostly on smaller prey, such as invertebrates, salamanders and frogs. The pit between the Copperhead's eye and nostril is an opening into a heat-sensitive organ that enables the snake to detect warm-blooded prey in the dark or track them along the forest floor.

Copperhead

The cold winds of November signal that the herpetological year is coming to a close. Most amphibian and reptile species are now in hibernation, well hidden in underground animal burrows, or tucked in rock or log crevices, or simply buried in the mud beneath wetlands. However, I know that I won't have too long to wait before I am again pulling on my waders, charging my flashlights, and heading out into the Delaware wilds to begin a new year observing the fascinating lives of Delaware's amphibians and reptiles.

(Following pages) Eastern Fence Lizard

Add together the more than 1,500 species of plants and 300 plus species of birds as well as all of the amphibians, reptiles and fish and you get a very large number and variety of species in Delaware. Take that number – whatever it is – and double it or maybe triple it and that may be approximately how many insects we have in Delaware. The truth is, no one knows for sure how many insects we have here.

For **Wild Delaware** I have focused on just a few of the more visually interesting insects. Looking like a Jurassic Period survivor, this Hellgrammite (right) is the larva stage of the Dobsonfly and is

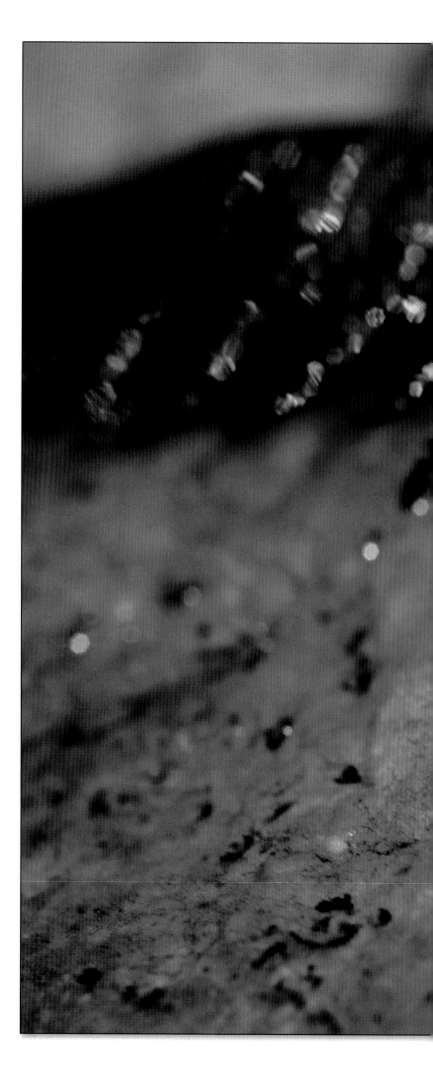

alive and well in White Clay Creek near Newark where it feeds on the larvae of other insects. If you find one of these guys under a rock beware of those pain-inducing pincers. After a couple of years of living underwater as larvae, Hellgrammites crawl onto land and pupate in a cocoon over the winter emerging in the spring as a Dobsonfly to mate and lay eggs. Seven days after emerging, the Dobsonfly dies.

Since 1974 the Ladybug (above) has been the official Delaware insect. Actually a beetle, Ladybugs eat aphids which are considered pests in gardens and farm fields.

(Left) Ladybug   •   Hellgrammite

(Left) Peregrine Falcon • Brown Pelicans

(Left) Northern Gannet • Herring Gulls

Ring-billed Gulls • (right) American Oystercatchers

It is amazing what you learn about wildlife behavior when you spend endless hours peering into their life through a telephoto lens.

For example, Snow geese always flap three times when stretching their wings. If you know this and you see the first flap you know you have a couple of seconds to frame and focus for the next two flaps (see pages 232 to 233).

When Red Fox are hunting it is all but impossible to distract them. Many times I have been able to get so close to foxes concentrating intently on catching dinner they are oblivious to me (see page 34 and pages 36 - 37).

Much of the year wildlife is pretty wary and getting close requires stealth, patience and lots of camouflage. But there are two times – a feeding frenzy and mating season – when

you can essentially approach wildlife and they don't care. The Ring-billed Gulls (left) were fighting over a clump of Horseshoe Crab eggs while I photographed them from just a few feet away. That same afternoon Red Knot, Ruddy Turnstones and Semipalmated Sandpipers were so busy gorging on the eggs that they actually came too close for me to focus (see pages 56 – 59).

During mating season, birds can be a little squirrelly. This American Oystercatcher (above) spent the morning biting and squawking at potential suitors that got too close to his mate.

My favorite display of wild behavior was watching a flock of Greater Yellowlegs (see pages 90 – 91) go through their mating ritual. One would chase another and they would reverse positions and chase each other back again. There seemed to be no rhyme or reason but I know there was.

Ruddy Turnstone • (Right) Herring Gull • (Following pages) Herring Gull

"We cannot win
this battle to save
species and
environments
without forging an
emotional bond
between ourselves
and nature as well -
for we will not
fight to save what
we do not love."

—Stephen Jay Gould

Black-necked Stilt
(Preceding pages) Herring Point,
Cape Henlopen State Park

"Though men now possess the power to dominate and exploit every corner of the natural world, nothing in that fact implies that they have the right or the need to do so."

—Edward Abbey

Snowy Egret

(Left) Clapper Rail • Short-billed Dowitchers

Greater Yellowlegs

Greater Yellowlegs

"It is not
enough to
understand the
natural world;
the point is to
defend and
preserve it."

—Edward Abbey

Honey Bee

"When one
tugs at a single
thing in nature;
he finds it
attached to
the rest of the
world."

–John Muir

Black and Yellow Garden Spider (Argiope aurantia) • (Following pages) Seaside Dragonlet

Monarch Butterfly

"We are still in transition from the notion of man as master of the earth to the notion of man as a part of it."

—Wallace Stegner

"Plans to
protect air and
water, wilderness
and wildlife are
in fact plans to
protect man."

—Unknown

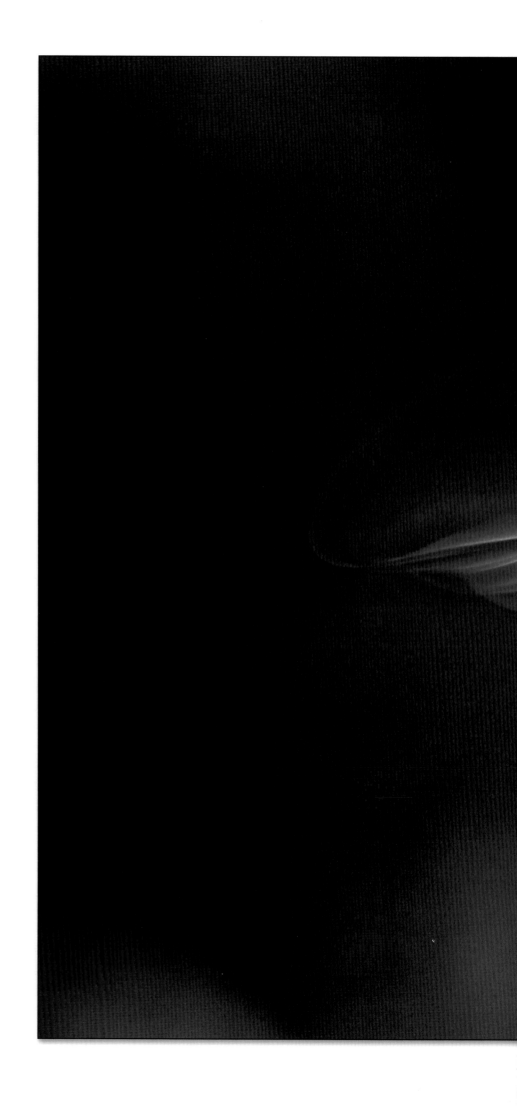

Ruby-throated Hummingbird • (Following pages) River Otter pups

American Goldfinch

"There is a way that nature speaks, that land speaks. Most of the time we are simply not patient enough, quiet enough to pay attention to the story."

–Linda Hogan

Kentucky Warbler

Canada Warbler

Northern Mockingbird

Northern Waterthrush

Acadian Flycatcher

Red-eyed Vireo

Blue Jay

White-tailed Deer fawn • (Right, Following pages and Preceding pages) White-tailed Deer

(Left) Pileated Woodpecker • Northern Flicker

(Left) House Sparrow • Carolina Wren • (Following pages) Diamondback Terrapin

Eastern Tiger Salamander • (Following pages) Barking Treefrog

"The human
spirit needs
places where
nature has not
been rearranged
by the hand
of man."

–Unknown

"Only those people that have directly experienced the wetlands that line the shore ... can appreciate their mystic qualities. The beauty of rising mists at dusk, the ebb and flow of the tides, the merging of fresh and salt waters...."

Governor's Task Force on Marine and Coastal Affairs
"Delaware: Wetlands," 1972

Green-winged Teal and Northern Pintail

tooth-like serrations for gripping slippery fish, earning them the nickname "sawbill."

Nearby, red-throated loons employ their dagger bills in a similar manner. Loons power their dives, as do ducks, grebes and cormorants, exclusively with their feet — they do not flap their wings underwater. In the case of loons, this need for foot power has forced an evolutionary compromise.

Loons' legs are set far back on their bodies, providing a lot of power underwater, but rendering them unable to walk on land. If a loon lands on the ground, it's stuck. Its heavy body requires a long, watery runway to become airborne again.

Most of the year, this is a good bargain. Loons simply

Red-breasted Merganser

live on the water. If you see a loon on the beach, it's either sick or injured.

The difficulty comes in the breeding season. Eggs must be laid and incubated and seawater is an inhospitable substrate. So is the beach — anywhere a loon could clamber to would be either too vulnerable to tide, or so far from shore as to render the parents helpless.

So loons must leave, the red-throated heading north to tundra ponds, where nests can be concealed right at the water's edge. But as soon as they can, loons return to big water.

On the beach itself, you'll find gulls, including the ring-billed gull, known to ornithologists as none

other than *Larus delawarensis*, which translates as "Gull of Delaware." Most likely named after the river, not the state, the species was first described in 1851 by George Ord, a resident of Philadelphia. But then again, our state is itself named after the river and bay, themselves named for a colonial governor of Virginia.

Ring-billed gulls, along with their larger cousins, herring gulls and great black-backed gulls, liven the winter, when summer residents like terns have mostly headed south. Their willingness to scavenge and their tolerance of human activity have allowed them to survive our winters in increasing numbers. You'll never see a tern picking through trash at a landfill, but gulls have made a major industry of it. You'll also find birders picking through the gulls, wherever they congregate, hoping to discover some far-flung stray from the north.

Look farther out toward the winter horizon, or take the Cape May-Lewes ferry across the mouth of Delaware Bay, and you'll see a bird that many tourists mistake for a gull, the northern gannet. Sure, they're large, black and white, and ocean-going, but they make gulls seem clunky and sluggish, like lumbering cargo planes overtaken by sleek fighter jets.

Gannets have a density of feathers that makes them appear luxuriantly smooth and plush — a pleasing aspect shared by loons, swans and waxwings, to name three. They always seem sleek and well groomed. No doubt this abundant feathering serves them well as insulation, too.

While gulls pick at the water's surface, gannets fold up into feathered darts, then shoot underwater, often zooming past their prey, which they snag as they swim back towards the surface. It's a beautiful performance.

Gannets breed in a few huge colonies that cling to seaside cliffs off Quebec and Newfoundland, where huge seasonal runs of capelin and other fish fuel their reproductive efforts. Winters, they spend at sea, with especially large numbers in our area in late fall and early spring.

But it's not as if the ocean is the only place where birds are active in the winter. By February, a number of our birds are already incubating, including great horned owls and bald eagles. It seems almost unbelievable on a bitter winter night, when the cold dry air instantly chills any exposed skin, that these birds are able to keep their eggs from freezing in their drafty treetop nests. But like so many improbable behaviors, its persistence is the proof of its success.

Winter is a good time to look for birds of prey. Northern harriers quarter over the fields, their somewhat owl-like faces gathering sound from the grasses, trying to discriminate the rustling caused by a vole from that caused by the wind. Red-tailed hawks are often abundant along forest edges, even hunting the shoulders and median strips of our highways.

In the marshes, stalwart great blue herons and clapper rails haunt the creeks, remaining with us even when so many of their brethren have departed for points south.

Forest birding is at its slowest in the colder months, but a bracing walk can still yield a nice variety of permanent resident birds, including northern cardinal, tufted titmouse and even pileated woodpecker, a species that draws oohs and aahs from all who see it. You've got to be pretty stony to not jump just a little when one of these latter-day pterodactyls sails by. It's an experience that is becoming increasingly common as forests mature, not only in protected parks and refuges, but even in aging subdivisions where the wild-looking pileated has become more than an occasional visitor.

Surviving the winter woods does require some ingenuity. Cardinals and titmice crack or hammer open seeds, while woodpeckers dig into wood for dormant grubs. A few land birds join us only for the winter, with dark-eyed juncoes being a prime example. Come April, these snowbirds, just as the song says, spread their tiny wings and fly away.

But in birding terms, April is well into spring. By the end of February, ducks are already crowding the marshes, most of them preparing for migrations that will take them far to our north and west. Northern pintail, northern shovelers, green-winged teal and a generous handful of other species flock to Bombay Hook and Prime Hook national wildlife refuges. It's a

great time to watch for courtship behavior, as the drakes display for the hens, bobbing and weaving with an abandon and an ardor that any observer of human behavior will instantly recognize.

The American black duck is one duck species you may see that will remain to breed here. It's not the showiest of its tribe, but it's worth special attention. Unlike its mid-continent cousin, the mallard, whose handsome, green-headed males contrast sharply with their well-camouflaged mates, black ducks are nearly unisex. Both the drake and the hen exhibit the same coaly body plumage, set off by silvery-white wing linings that flash like mirrors when the birds flush.

This marsh-loving duck is itself beloved of

Osprey

waterfowlers and other wildlife enthusiasts, many of whom are worried about its future. To put it delicately, ducks aren't the most selective birds when it comes to mating and our American black ducks are being genetically overrun by those green-headed mallards.

It used to be that the two forms were reproductively isolated, with mallards breeding primarily in prairie pothole wetlands of interior North America and black ducks to the east, but time and waterfowl management practices have eroded those barriers.

It's increasingly difficult to find black ducks that don't show some evidence of mallard heritage — a brush of shiny green across the face, or a bit of gray to the body. Perhaps, as some contend, these two forms

aren't fully differentiated species. Still, it's hard not to hope that the black duck will survive as a distinct type.

March is a time of anxious waiting for Delaware birders. Many of our winter water birds are heading north and their summer replacements can at times seem painfully slow in returning. But that's our lot in spring. It takes awhile for that huge bowl of saltwater off our coast to warm up.

Still, the birds come faithfully. Tree swallows and egrets sometimes seem to regret their haste in returning when late-season chills descend, but temperatures usually rise quickly. Piping plovers return to the few protected beaches where they still successfully nest.

By April, our species diversity is growing daily. Warblers, a group of songbirds that seem to many to be the zenith of avian evolution, begin to return in numbers. Many, though not all, are brightly colored; most are good singers.

Moreover, they have an intensity, a lively energy about them that gives them a charisma well beyond their small size.

Camouflaged Louisiana water thrushes arrive early in the month. Their rich songs echo over the noise of the streams where they forage. It takes a few more weeks for the brilliant yellow Kentucky warbler, with his jet black later-Elvis sideburns, to return.

Sometime toward the end of April, most local birders make a pilgrimage to the cypresses and pinelands of Sussex County, perhaps visiting Trap Pond State Park or the Great Cypress Swamp. It's a springtime tonic for the many who appreciate nature. Leaves are budding, but not so large that they make birds hard to see. And even when they stay just beyond sight, the songs of birds are everywhere, their territorial and breeding imperatives tumbling from countless thousands of tiny throats.

Things get more hectic in May. The newly arrived breeders are joined by a flood tide of transients that grace us only for a few weeks each year. The woods around White Clay Creek and Brandywine Creek state parks come to resemble an unending series of Christmas mornings, crowds of birders turning out to

Piping Plover

see what presents the day has brought them.

Most songbirds migrate at night. Wind conditions tend to be more stable then and hungry predators are few. Birds take off just after dusk and ascend, gearing up for a marathon they will repeat many times in the space of just a few weeks. At dawn, if the weather has cooperated, the tired migrants look for a suitable patch of habitat in which to feed and rest. As soon as their reserves are replenished and the weather looks good, they climb once more into the darkness.

In the first two weeks of May, bird diversity in Delaware reaches its annual peak. Dedicated birders engaging in 24-hour endurance tests called Big Days during the height of May migration can hope to see and hear almost 200 species within Delaware in a single calendar day, well over half of what a very active birder might hope to find here in a year. It's a rush, in many dimensions, for both birds and birders.

Even as the warbler migration dies down, the stage is set for the arrival of a new set of migrants. It's a big production, with many fine players, but the stars of the show are undoubtedly red knots.

Not only are red knots sumptuously beautiful, they're athletic, too, undertaking a hemisphere-spanning annual migration from Patagonia to the

Arctic Archipelago. Moreover, their survival is in considerable doubt, in large part due to the decimated numbers of horseshoe crabs spawning along Delaware Bay, a local connection of truly global import.

The knots time their northward migration so that they arrive in the mid-Atlantic in mid-May, just before the peak breeding activity of horseshoe crabs, when thousands of these dun-green creatures clamber onto our shorelines, depositing millions of eggs and inadvertently turning the beaches into a wild caviar buffet.

Red knots aren't the only species attuned to the

Red Knot

annual provision of easy calories. A dozen or more types of shorebirds show up specifically for this feast, as do laughing gulls, diamondback terrapins and many others. I can only imagine the hordes of fish and other marine creatures that gorge on washed-out crab eggs on the underwater side of the beach.

But the red knot trumps all of them, a poster child if ever there was one, and a species that our children will rightfully never forgive us for losing, should we be so foolish as to allow that to happen.

Once Memorial Day has passed, activity seems almost to decline. It's a deceptive appearance, for now

the heavy lifting of the year is truly underway for most of our birds. From the fields to forests to the beaches, just about everything is nesting. Harried parents have demanding mouths to feed; though summer seems long and slow, in reality they are on a schedule that would stress out an advertising executive.

The most demanding events of the year, for many species, all cluster in spring in summer. Migrate north. Claim territory. Find a mate. Nest. Molt. Migrate south. No wonder that most long-distance migrant songbirds have life expectancies of less than five years.

Contrast that with many larger, more sedentary species like gulls or eagles, who may well live into their twenties.

For the migrants, time is exceedingly short. The Fourth of July may seem rather early in the summer but about then we see our first migrant birds heading south. Usually, it's shorebirds, often the lesser yellowlegs, that return first. By August, birds and birders are deep into autumn.

Fall is a great time to return to the coastal refuges, but be sure to bring some protection from the biting flies and mosquitoes, which can be truly oppressive when the breeze dies. In addition to viewing the regular migrants, fall offers the opportunity to discover stray species that have wandered or been blown off course, something that just about every birder enjoys, some to the point of mania.

While spring birding has an unbeatable excitement, the migration from September through November has a majesty and emotional heft that even May cannot match — and the weather is as fine and dependable as spring's is fickle.

The arithmetic is undeniable, too. Think about it: even averaging out for the nest failures and adult casualties, for every pair of adult birds that began the breeding season, a clan of anywhere from three to six or more is, one hopes, heading south. There are simply more birds to be seen.

Never mind that the first year is also by far the most perilous; those swollen numbers will be thinned considerably by winter's end. On a fine October day, it's hard to think of anything but abundance.

Just about anywhere you look in the thick of fall, you'll find birds. The woods and fields are filled with songbirds, beginning with warblers and finishing with sparrows. Raptors follow the Piedmont hills as well as the coastline southward. The salt marshes, as usual, are full of everything from shorebirds to ducks.

Beginning in November, they also fill up with flocks of snow geese. Even if you couldn't see their tumbling, black and white bodies spilling from the sky, zigzagging down into the water, just the noise is amazing — a crescendo of raw organic sound that moves some to tears and others to earplugs. Add in the visual, which — as evidenced in the photographs here — is really quite lovely and you can understand why many hundreds of people who would never think of themselves as bird watchers still go out each fall to look at geese.

Snow geese are birds important enough to have detractors — a significant number of people consider them pests; not only farmers, who regard them with the same kind of alarm with which they might greet a flock of flying lawnmowers, but also habitat managers and other wildlife enthusiasts who worry about the impact that so many grazing bills are having on our salt marsh. Even on the expansive tundra of Nunuvat, Canada, the breeding grounds for most of our snow geese, the species is viewed with mounting apprehension, as it appears to be overrunning its habitat.

Certainly, numbers of snow geese have increased dramatically in recent decades. As little as 50 years ago, the hordes we see today would have been unthinkable. So what accounts for the increase? Changes in hunting pressure for one. Snow geese were entirely protected from hunting for more than half of the 20th century, their numbers having been driven perilously low by

overhunting in the 19th. While hunting resumed in the 1970s, it hasn't kept pace with the snow goose population.

Further, the role of climate change and evolving agricultural practices is unsurprisingly the subject of much debate. But whether you applaud them or curse them, snow geese are an integral part of our natural environment and a true spectacle.

With the return of the snow geese, the brant, the loons, the gannets and all the others who will ride out the winter with us, the birding year in Delaware draws to a close. There are Christmas Counts to be

Mute Swan

taken and the data submitted. Year lists and others are tabulated. Stories of the year's great finds, and the great finds from years past are told and retold.

Winter hasn't really taken hold yet and already, the birds and their watchers alike are turning their attention to the seasons to come. In a few short weeks, the breast feathers of eagles and owls will warm the eggs that hold the promise of next year's young.

It's an annual cycle that seems richer and more remarkable each time you experience it. If you haven't given birding in Delaware a try, I urge you to. It's simply too good to miss.

(Following pages) Red-tailed Hawk

(Left) immature Bald Eagle   •   Bald Eagle   •   (Following pages) Osprey

Eastern Screech-Owl • (Right) Great Horned Owl

Eastern Gray Squirrel • (Right) Eastern Cottontail

Long-Legged Fly (*chrysosoma*)

THE SCIENCE OF NATURE

Jean L. Woods

Dr. Jean L. Woods is director of collections at the Delaware Museum of Natural History.

Trays of shells and eggs — items of beauty from the natural world of Delaware. Who hasn't picked up a shell or feather or leaf that caught their eye? The eggs and shells pictured here are part of the more than 370,000 specimens in the collections of the Delaware Museum of Natural History. At the museum, these objects are more than just items of beauty, they are tools of science and education. They are used in many ways to increase our understanding of the natural world of Delaware.

The specimens in our collections are a record of the biodiversity of Earth, both past and present. They come

from Delaware and also from the farthest corners of the Earth. Museum specimens are at the root of one of the most basic aspects of the study of biodiversity: the naming and description of species. Specimens provide scientific proof of the distribution of species around the world. While many species can be readily identified by sight, some shells, insects and even birds are so hard to identify that they must be compared to specimens in a museum to confirm their identification. Without named species and knowledge of their distribution, we have no baseline data for conservation efforts. Scientists also use the specimens in our collections in many other ways, such as the study of evolution, ecology, geographic variation, and even migration.

As a scientist, I place a high value on the importance of the collections to scientific research, but the collections also serve as

a tool to help people learn about the natural world of Delaware. Have you ever wished that a kinglet would hold still so you could get a good look at it? Or maybe you'd like to see a downy woodpecker and a hairy woodpecker side by side? Students in the museum's bird identification classes have just that opportunity, using specimens from our collections. While nothing can replace the experience of going out into nature to observe birds, the chance to study specimens up close can really help a birder learn their birds. Children in the museum's school tours even have a chance to touch a real specimen — an experience sure to open their eyes to the wonders of the natural world.

Bird watchers in Delaware are probably familiar with *Birds of Delaware* (Hess *et al.*, 2000), which contains a comprehensive review of what is known about the birds of our state. Many of the accounts refer to birds and eggs that were collected in Delaware. These specimens document the history of birds in the state, particularly for birds that are no longer found here. Other specimen records are from time periods in the history of Delaware when there were no standardized surveys like the Christmas Bird Count, and thus represent one of our best ways of knowing about birds during these historic periods. As we watch the natural habitats of Delaware being changed by humans and face the likelihood of climate change on a global scale, the specimens we continue to add to the collections will provide the basis for understanding change in the future.

The specimens in our collections also inspire art. Bird carvers, sculptors, painters and even photographers use our collections regularly. While looking at specimens can never replace the artist's firsthand experience of the natural world, they can learn much about size, shape and color from our specimens. You can be sure that the artists who illustrated every field guide you own spent time in a museum collection. The staff here greatly enjoyed Kevin's visit to the collection. For me, the most fascinating part of it was discovering which specimens caught Kevin's eye, compared to my favorites and those specimens that I thought would attract him.

You might think that in a small state like Delaware, we already know almost everything about the animals living here. Yet even for the species that are most common, there are still things to be discovered. There are also almost certainly animals living here that we don't even know about — tiny snails or insects. As the museum continues to build its collections, we are looking to the future, the next generation of scientists who will use our specimens in their research and the many other people who will learn from our specimens. We hope many of them will be inspired to go out and discover the wild side of Delaware.

songbird eggs (left side from top), Orchard Oriole, Red-winged Blackbird, Eastern Towhee, Northern Cardinal, American Robin, Gray Catbird (right side from top), Blue Jay, Carolina Chickadee, Song Sparrow, Field Sparrow, Chipping Sparrow, Seaside Sparrow

...e spurius
DATE 30 May 193_
_ECTOR Court & Ball
_LITY U__ ___ New Alexandr__
MARK _INCUB._
_IN SE_ _DENT_

_DATE
LOCALITY F_ _ndo
SET MARK_ _n
NO. IN SET_ _d*
__642

Agelaius ph___ _Ap__
DMNH 1_

1925
_L_ _rascosa Creek_
_S_ _B. fresh to
M_ _embryos
IDENTITY_ _flushed_
_NNH 10080

_uxed___ 1403
___
DMNH 8792

_ECTC
_lity
_MARK
N SET _IDENT_
DMNH 8-

_din__ _lis
_9 _N_
DM__ __8895

Spizella pusilla
DATE 30 JUNE 1940
ECTOR Court &
_ALITY Maryla__ _, Aquasco
ET MARK 5240 _. fresh
NO. IN SET 4_ _TY flushe_
DMNH 8_

*_lus migr_*
_NO._ _1943
_ta. F_ _Tuxed_
_ET 4

Sp___ *Serin_*
NO._ _DATE
COL_ _ON Nichol_
LOC_ _Maryland: Montg_ _Co., near
SE_ _1/4_ _Pooleville
_ INCUB. fresh
N_ _IDENTITY "L__
DMNH S_

DATE _ 1453
DJ N_ _ Tuxedo
rth Ca _ Co
63/_
_ET 4
DMNH _

_DATE
DMNH 8156

SPECIES { Larus delawarensis
Ring-billed Gull

DEL. MUS. NAT. HIST.
656

A. O. U. NO. 54   DATE 5-16-1915
SET MARK 110-3   INCUBATION Advanced
EGGS IN SET Thre...   IDENTIFICATI...
LOCALITY ...at Salt...
NEST a ...tc...

COLLEC...

① ... ...

THE OOLOGICAL COLLECTION
OF
E. FIFIELD

DEL. MUS. NAT. HIST.
630

...ARE MARKED
...INDEX

...Herring G...
...argentat...
...chang...
...tion a...

⑤

A.O...
...ade...
...water.
...aud Sikkin

⑨

...Collection of...
Nam...
...tificati...

⑩

A.O.U. No...
...et Mark...
...of Egg...

1. Ring-billed Gull   2. Fosters Tern   3. Black Tern   4. Black Skimmer   5. Herring Gull   6. Laughing Gull   7. Killdeer
8. American Woodcock   9. Common Tern   10. Spotted Sandpiper   11. Black-necked Stilt   12. Piping Plover   13. Least Tern

(Left) Green Heron • Northern Red-bellied Cooter (turtle) in Duckweed • (Preceding pages) Great Blue Heron

"Sometimes I
do get to places
when God's
ready to have
someone click
the shutter."

–Ansel Adams

Great Blue Heron

"The most unhappy thing
about conservation is
that it is never permanent.
If we save a priceless

woodland today, it is

threatened from another

quarter tomorrow."

- Marjory Stoneman Douglas

(Left) Tree Swallows · Barn Swallow

"The battle for conservation will go on endlessly. It is part of the universal warfare between right and wrong."

–John Muir

Eastern Hog-nosed Snake • (Following pages) Copperhead

Rough Green Snake • (Right) Eastern Kingsnake

THE FURRY SIDE OF THE FIRST STATE

Derek Stoner

Derek Stoner is a lifelong outdoorsman who enjoys tracking, photographing and studying mammals. A naturalist for the Delaware Nature Society, he leads field trips in search of mammals and teaches the mammal course for the Naturalist Certification Series at Ashland Nature Center in Hockessin.

A boyhood fascination with road kill sparked my interest in mammals. I eventually realized, through my own non-scientific studies, that being able to identify week-old flattened mammary glands and extended young-rearing. What human mother cannot relate to the mother possum carrying her babies on her back?

Though small in size, Delaware is blessed with a great variety of mammals. From the tiniest (least shrew) to the largest (white-tailed deer), there is an abundance of mammalian life sharing our living space. Some animals, like the gray squirrel, are ubiquitous and familiar to all, while others, like the coyote, are scarce and mysterious.

Springtime can be a great time to look for mammals, and you may come across furry babies out exploring their new world. Dawn Webb, a licensed wildlife rehabilitator and manager of the DuPont Nature Center in Milford, notes that the two most common mammals brought to her are baby rabbits and gray squirrels. Fall and winter are ideal for mammal-watching, as cold weather makes

Eastern Gray Squirrel

possum just couldn't substitute for close encounters of the furred kind.

Inspired by amazing behavioral footage captured on television programs like *Wild America*, I desperately wanted to learn more about the mammals that lived in my backyard. While we didn't have bighorn sheep, wolves or musk ox lurking in my neighborhood, a multitude of squirrels, rabbits and groundhogs kept me entertained.

Today, working as a naturalist and educator, I find that many people share the same fascination with the mammals living in our region. After all, these are creatures that share our same features of hair,

hungry animals move more often through the barren landscape. Summertime, with lush plant growth and hot temperatures, often means mammals are hidden and resting during daylight hours.

While teaching classes about mammals, I often joke that you don't hear people say they are "going mammaling." To go out and expect to observe a variety of mammals going about their business is unrealistic. Many of our mammals are nocturnal, shy around humans and well-camouflaged — a sure recipe for difficult observing! The hours just after dawn or just before dusk, known as the crepuscular period, provide the best chance for observing mammal activity. Most

Sweet Gum leaf on Foxtail

Mute Swan • (Right) Tundra Swan

"Wild beasts and birds
are by right not the
property merely of the
people who are alive
today, but the property

of unknown generations,
whose belongings
we have no right to
squander."

- Theodore Roosevelt

(Left) Herring Gull • Ring-billed Gull • (Following pages) Canada goose

(Left) American Bittern • Short-billed Dowitcher • (Following pages) Double-crested Cormorant

Northern Shoveler

TRAP POND
& TRUSSUM POND

Jennifer Ackerman

The freshwater swamp in and around Trap Pond State Park looks more like a Southern bayou than the bottomside of Delaware. Delaware's first state park, Trap Pond hosts one of the northernmost stands of Bald Cypress in the country. The old mill pond and the park's surrounding 900 acres lie in the region once known as the Delaware Everglades, a 50,000-acre cypress swamp that supported trees well over 100 feet high and many centuries old. Few of the old-growth trees survive. Most went the way of shingles, posts and boats or were lost to peat fires that swept the area in 1930. Still, young cypresses grow tall and shaggy along the pond's margins and form thick swamps near its headwaters. The bulbous trunk of the tree stabilizes it in the soft mucky soils. The cone-shaped "knees," which now and then sprout from the roots and protrude from the water, help support the tree and carry oxygen to its flooded roots.

Though you can see the cypresses from points along the park's six miles of woodland paths, nothing beats wandering by boat through the maze of buttressed trunks and knees. A canoe trail leads from Trap Pond to Records Pond along the James Branch River, Delaware's best canoe stream. The clear, tea-colored waters of the James Branch flow through old stands of cypress, including one giant more than 500 years old and 33 feet in circumference. En route is a tiny place of wild beauty: Trussum Pond, where cypresses emerge from a black surface choked with white waterlilies and yellow-flowered spatterdock. This woodland swamp is hardly a shadow of the mature forest that grew here. Still it remains a small but essential remnant of the wet wilderness that once was.

Bald Cypress
(Following pages) Trussum Pond

Wilson's Snipe • (Following pages) Brant

"Only when the last tree has died, and the last river been poisoned, and the last fish been caught we will realize we cannot eat money."

–Cree Indian Proverb

Canada geese on Brandywine Creek

There's something magical about standing knee-deep in the wetlands of Prime Hook National Wildlife Refuge in the azure blue light just before sunrise. Goose music fills the air; there are thousands of snow geese in all directions, as far as I can see. Then suddenly, as if on cue, the honking stops and seconds later the air is filled with the rush of the wind from the wings of ten thousand snow geese launching into the sky all at once.

By January we have as many as 150,000 Snow geese – that's more than twice the human population of Wilmington, the state's largest city – filling our wetlands along the Delaware River and Bay.

While birdwatchers delight in seeing the huge flocks, wildlife managers trying to maintain habitat and farmers trying to grow winter wheat probably don't see Snow geese as a thing of beauty. When feeding, Snow geese tend to pull up vegetation by the roots. Farmers near the refuges, some armed with exploding shells for 12 gauge shotguns and automatically firing propane cannons, face a daily struggle keeping hordes of geese off their fields. By spring, it is easy to see acres of denuded brown spots in otherwise green winter wheat fields and know the Snow geese have won many battles.

I remember as recently as the early 1970s Snow geese were rare in Delaware. Then, just a few years later, by the late 1970s Snow geese were becoming common. Now, they are as ubiquitous in the winter sky as puffy, white clouds. No one can say with any certainty why their population mushroomed and why they chose Delaware as their winter home. Some argue that climate change is the cause and others speculate that changes in agricultural practices may be the reason.

As a photographer, these elegant birds compel me to pick up my camera and head into the salt marsh on cold winter mornings. There's something about the sheer number of these stark white birds filling the sky from one edge of the horizon to the other that reminds me of the glory days of African wildlife. While they are here now in vast numbers, there may be a day again soon where their migration patterns change and they leave Delaware. I'm sure the farmers and wildlife managers would be happy but I would miss the spectacle and sound of all those wings in the air.

(Preceding pages) Dunlin over Snow geese
(Left and to end of book) Snow geese